Cats, Cats, Cats

Long-Haired
Cat Breeds

by Christina Mia Gardeski

CAPSTONE PRESS
a capstone imprint

Pebble Plus is published by Capstone Press,
1710 Roe Crest Drive, North Mankato, Minnesota 56003
www.mycapstone.com

Library of Congress Cataloging-in-Publication Data
Cataloging-in-publication information is on file with the Library of Congress.
ISBN 978-1-5157-0959-6 (library binding)
ISBN 978-1-5157-1125-4 (ebook PDF)

Editorial Credits
Jaclyn Jaycox, editor; Philippa Jenkins, designer;
Pam Mitsakos, media researcher; Steve Walker, production specialist

Photo Credits
Shutterstock: Eric Isselee, 3, cover, backcover, Joanna22, 17, Oleksandr Schevchuk, 19, red rose,
design element throughout, Rob Hainer, 1, 7, Rosa Jay, 13, Russ Beinder, 11, Sergey Skleznev, 5,
Tatiana Makotra, 21, Trybex, 15; Thinkstock: MollyNZ, 9

Note to Parents and Teachers

The Cats, Cats, Cats set supports national science standards related to life
science. This book describes and illustrates long-haired cat breeds. The images
support early readers in understanding the text. The repetition of words and
phrases helps early readers learn new words. This book also introduces early
readers to subject-specific vocabulary words, which are defined in the Glossary
section. Early readers may need assistance to read some words and to use the
Table of Contents, Glossary, Read More, Internet Sites, Critical Thinking Using
the Common Core, and Index sections of the book.

Printed and bound in China
PO007732LEOF16

Table of Contents

Long-Haired Cats

Cats can be put into groups called breeds. There are almost 100 cat breeds. Some have long hair. Let's meet some of these sweet cats.

Himalayan

Himalayans have bright blue eyes. They have light coats. They have darker areas on their faces, ears, legs, and tails. The darker areas are called points.

Birman

Birmans look like Himalayans. They have light coats, points, and blue eyes. But Birmans also have white paws. Their silky fur does not mat easily.

Ragdoll

The Ragdoll is a gentle cat.

It relaxes when picked up.

It makes its body floppy like

a doll. This is how the Ragdoll

got its name.

Maine Coon

The Maine Coon is the state cat of Maine. It gets its name from the state and its tail. The Maine Coon's long, fluffy tail looks like a raccoon's tail.

Persian

Persians have a lot of soft fur.
The hairy ruff around their necks
looks like a lion's mane. Their
ruffs and fluffy bellies need to
be brushed often.

Norwegian Forest Cat

The Norwegian Forest Cat has two layers of fur. Its outer coat acts like a raincoat to keep the cat dry. The thick undercoat keeps the cat warm.

Turkish Angora

Turkish Angoras can be many colors or patterns. Some are just one color. Others have a striped coat. These playful cats welcome visitors to their homes.

Ragamuffin

Ragamuffins look a lot like Ragdolls. They have soft, thick fur. Most love to be petted. Ragamuffins are good friends to children and other pets. They are calm and trusting.

Glossary

breed—a group of the same kind of animals

coat—an animal's hair or fur

mane—long, thick hair growing around the necks of some animals; cats and horses have manes

mat—to form a lump of twisted hair

pattern—a repeated shape or form

points—dark patches of fur on an animal's face, ears, paws, or tail

ruff—long hairs growing around or on a cat's neck

undercoat—animal hair that grows under a long top layer of fur

Read More

Dash, Meredith. *Persian Cats*. Cats. Minneapolis: ABDO Kids, 2015.

Olson, Gillia M. *Pet Cats Up Close*. Pets Up Close. North Mankato, Minn.: Capstone Press, 2015.

Owen, Ruth. *American Longhairs*. Cats Are Cool. New York: PowerKids Press, 2014.

Internet Sites

FactHound offers a safe, fun way to find Internet sites related to this book. All of the sites on FactHound have been researched by our staff.

Here's all you do:

Visit *www.facthound.com*

Type in this code: 9781515709596

Check out projects, games and lots more at
www.capstonekids.com

Critical Thinking Using the Common Core

- Some long-haired cat breeds have points. What are points? (Craft and Structure)

- Choose two long-haired cat breeds mentioned in this book. How are they the same? How are they different? (Key Ideas and Details)

- Which long-haired cat is your favorite? Why? (Integration of Knowledge and Ideas)

Index